Hello, Family Members,

Learning to read is one of the most important accomplishments of early childhood. **Hello Reader!** books are designed to help children become skilled readers who like to read. Beginning readers learn to read by remembering frequently used words like "the," "is," and "and"; by using phonics skills to decode new words; and by interpreting picture and text clues. These books provide both the stories children enjoy and the structure they need to read fluently and independently. Here are suggestions for helping your child *before*, *during*, and *after* reading:

Before
- Look at the cover and pictures and have your child predict what the story is about.
- Read the story to your child.
- Encourage your child to chime in with familiar words and phrases.
- Echo read with your child by reading a line first and having your child read it after you do.

During
- Have your child think about a word he or she does not recognize right away. Provide hints such as "Let's see if we know the sounds" and "Have we read other words like this one?"
- Encourage your child to use phonics skills to sound out new words.
- Provide the word for your child when more assistance is needed so that he or she does not struggle and the experience of reading with you is a positive one.
- Encourage your child to have fun by reading with a lot of expression . . . like an actor!

After
- Have your child keep lists of interesting and favorite words.
- Encourage your child to read the books over and over again. Have him or her read to brothers, sisters, grandparents, and even teddy bears. Repeated readings develop confidence in young readers.
- Talk about the stories. Ask and answer questions. Share ideas about the funniest and most interesting characters and events in the stories.

I do hope that you and your child enjoy this book.

— Francie Alexander
   Reading Specialist,
   Scholastic's Learning Ventures

To Paul and Andrew and Russell
and Jordana — kids with brilliant smiles!
—G.S.

To Maggie's teeth: thanks for lighting up
her smile.
—G.N.

The editors would like to thank Dr. Lawrence Golub
for his expertise.

ISBN: 0-439-20642-1

Text copyright © 2001 by Gina Shaw.
Illustrations copyright © 2001 by Greg Neri.
All rights reserved. Published by Scholastic Inc.
SCHOLASTIC, HELLO READER, CARTWHEEL BOOKS and associated
logos are trademarks and/or registered trademarks of Scholastic Inc.

Library of Congress Cataloging-in-Publication Data
Shaw, Gina.
    Hooray for teeth! / by Gina Shaw ; illustrated by Greg Neri.
      p.   cm.—(Hello reader! Level 2)
    ISBN 0-439-20642-1 (pbk.)
    1. Teeth—Juvenile literature. [1. Teeth.] I. Neri, Greg, ill. II. Title.
III. Series.
QM311 .S47   2000
591.4—dc21   00-036541

20 19 18 17 16   06 07

Printed in the U.S.A.   23
First printing, January 2001

HOORAY FOR TEETH!

by Gina Shaw
Illustrated by Greg Neri

Hello Reader! Science — Level 2

SCHOLASTIC INC. Cartwheel B·O·O·K·S ®
New York Toronto London Auckland Sydney
Mexico City New Delhi Hong Kong

Many living things have teeth.
Elephants, zebras, and cows do.

Crocodiles, fish, and apes do, too.

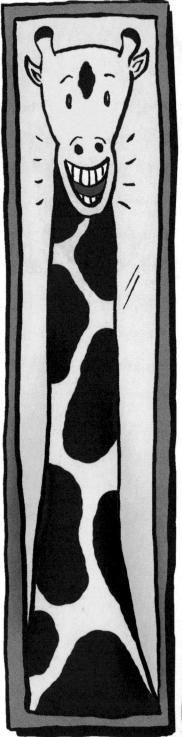

Cats and dogs
and lions,
hyenas, giraffes,
and sheep do.

A very special person has teeth, too.
That person is . . .

A shark has many rows of teeth.
The first row stands up.
The next rows lie flat.
If a shark loses a tooth
in the front row, one of the teeth
from the back row fills
the empty space.
A shark gets new teeth
throughout its life.

You have one row of teeth
on the top of your mouth and
one row on the bottom.

Snakes have teeth that curve
back toward the throat.
The rattlesnake has two long,
sharp teeth.

These teeth are called **fangs**.
Fangs have holes in them.
Poison comes out of the
holes when a rattlesnake
bites another animal.

Your teeth stand straight
up and down.

Beavers, rats, and mice have
teeth that grow all the time.
These animals use their teeth
to gnaw wood, bark, and nuts.

This wears down their teeth
so their teeth stay short.

The teeth of the walrus grow
all the time, too.
But the walrus doesn't gnaw
on wood.
So its teeth get longer.
These teeth are called **tusks**.

The walrus uses its tusks
to pull its huge body
out of the water.

Your teeth don't grow
all the time.
But you get two sets of teeth
during your life —

baby teeth

and grown-up teeth.

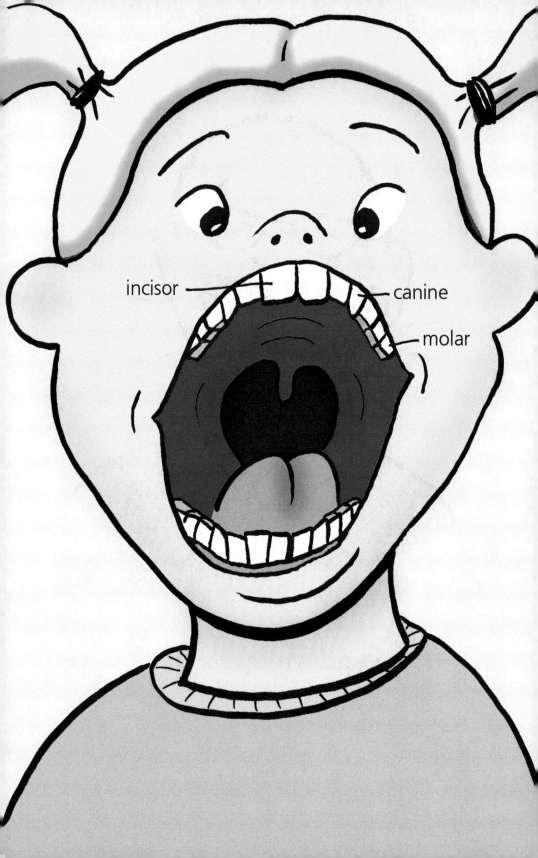

Different types of teeth are used for different things.

Square, sharp teeth in the front of the mouth are called **incisors**. They are used for biting food.

Long, pointy teeth, called **canines**, are used for tearing food.

Flat teeth at the back of the mouth are called **molars**. They are used for grinding food.

Some animals — horses,
giraffes, and sheep —
have large, flat teeth
because they only eat plants.

Plants are hard to chew.
If these animals had small teeth
like yours, their teeth would
wear out quickly.

Some animals have two or more
kinds of teeth.
Dogs and cats have incisors
for biting into food.
They have molars
for chewing food.
They also have canines
for tearing food.

Lions and tigers have
incisors, molars, and
canines, too.

And you have incisors, canines,
and molars!
These teeth help you eat many
different foods —
meats, fish, fruits,
and vegetables.
Right now, you probably have
20 teeth in your mouth.
You have 10 upper teeth and
10 lower teeth.

As you grow older, your baby teeth will fall out. Why?

So there will be room
for your grown-up teeth.

Here's what happens.

Inside your gums, grown-up teeth grow underneath your baby teeth. The roots of your baby teeth slowly start to dissolve.

As the root dissolves, the baby tooth becomes loose.

You can wiggle it with your finger or your tongue.

A grown-up tooth is pushing up
under the loose tooth.
It keeps pushing and pushing.
Soon, the baby tooth will fall out.
This will make room for the new,
grown-up tooth.
The new tooth will be bigger
than the baby tooth was.

When all your new teeth come in, you should have 32 teeth.
There will be 16 teeth on the top and 16 teeth on the bottom.

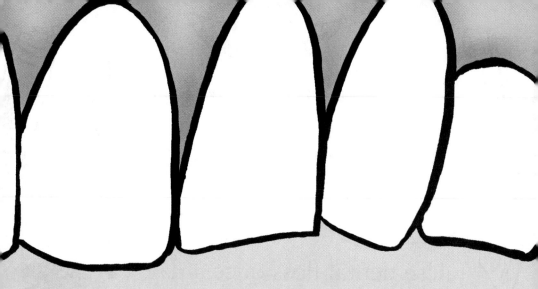

You will have your grown-up teeth
for a very long time.
So, you should take good care
of them.

Good Teeth Tips

Brush your teeth after every meal.

Use dental floss once a day.

Don't eat too many foods filled with sugar.

Eat healthy snacks — fresh fruits and vegetables, cheese, and nuts.

Visit your dentist every six months.

Drink plenty of milk and water.

If you do all of this, you will have healthy teeth and a bright smile!